Poetic License
Reflections and Renderings

Poetic License
Reflections and Renderings

Lawrence L. Schwartz

IPBOOKS.net
Infinite Possibilities

Infinite Possibilities
New York • http://www.IPBooks.net

Published by IPBooks,
Queens, NY 2022
Online at: www.IPBooks.net

Cover Photo by Maurice Galimidi: *Trees Reflected in Water* (2017), used with permission and gratitude.

Cover layout by Kathy Kovacic, Blackthorn Studio.
Interior design and layout by Noel S. Morado

ISBN: 978-1-956864-24-3

Contents

CONTENTS

Acknowledgments

My gratitude goes to the myriad of teachers, mentors, friends, fellow students, and my parents, who have encouraged me throughout my life to keep writing, and who have been appreciative of my efforts over a period of many years. A special thanks to my old college dorm-mate, Maurice Galimidi, for providing the cover photo of trees reflected in water. Thanks go too for the inspiration gained from gurus, yoga and meditation teachers, swamis, and philosophers—East and West—of varying schools of thought, from ancient rishis and yogis to recent or current mystics and visionaries of the modern era, including the nondual approaches of both *Advaita Vedanta* and *Kashmir Shaivism*. With great appreciation to All Faiths Seminary International, its founder Rabbi Joseph H. Gelberman, and its entire faculty and student body since 2011, for keeping me active in expressing and engaging myself in spiritual dialogue and interactions from year to year. I would be remiss not to also mention my parents-in-law who were instrumental in establishing IPBooks as the publishing platform that it is.

Finally, I am forever grateful to my beloved wife Tamar, who has truly been a constant "Rendering and Reflection" of Love in my life for the past 31 years, and without whom I often wonder whether I would do anything at all.

Introduction

I've decided to limit my commentary to these introductory remarks. I'm publishing this book, at least in part, because of the large number of people who have asked me to do so over the years, and, and in part, because it feels good to have finally consolidated enough pieces to be able to publish a book, however small.

I have been told by some people that my poems say things that they never thought could be expressed in words. Some folks, on the other hand, have said that at least some of these are not really poems at all because they say things *too outrightly*—not couched in enough metaphor or imagery for them to be considered poetry.

I have decided to split the difference and call them "poetic renderings." I leave it to the reader to decide whether to call them poems. I didn't write them to live up to any poetic standard. They have come when something inwardly arises and insists that *it is time.* Something needs to be expressed, not as an essay, lecture, or discussion, but in a form for which I feel the need to "take poetic license."

Each comes out of a process wherein a little itch of inspiration rises up and grows into something that will not rest until the last line has been perceived as such by me, and then a sigh of relief bids me that it is finished, and it's time to rest from the writing.

Often, I am grateful for what comes through in this process, even if sometimes unsure whether a piece will have value for anyone else. At such times the validation or feedback from others can be a welcome acknowledgement of something too fresh or too recent for me to yet have a clear perspective on.

A *Little History*

When I was in third and fourth grade, I used to pass around a little memo pad to my classmates with a list of the names of several animals on the page, and a note to fellow students saying: "Which one should I write a poem about?" Someone would pass it back to me with the name of an animal circled, and I would write a little rhyming ditty about whatever animal was suggested.

I remember that once it came back with three different animals circled, and so one of my earliest remembered pieces became: "Elephant, Anteater, and Skunk."

> *The elephant eats things with his nose,*
> *The anteater's tongue slurps up junk,*
> *But let us not forget*
> *The strangeness of the skunk.*
>
> *The anteater has a long, long tongue,*
> *The elephant's nose is a trunk,*
> *But let us not forget*
> *The strangeness of the skunk!*

It was not my best or cleverest poem but it got a great reaction from my classmates and thus became the single one of those early animal rhymes that sticks in my memory.

Perhaps it was my father's penchant for quoting Ogden Nash's witty little animal poems at every opportunity, and also probably the influence of my grandfather, "Papa" (Benjamin Kleinman), who used to always write personalized little rhymes on all his birthday and holiday greeting cards to family members—and perhaps my appreciation and affection for Dr. Seuss as a youngster—but such poetry became an integral part of my childhood identity.

In the Summer of 1968, when I was 12 years old, we moved to a new neighborhood, and I started junior high school in an unfamiliar place with unfamiliar classmates. I was never much of an athlete, could not dribble a basketball, and had never been much good at any sports. In the adolescent student culture of a boys' gym class, any guy who couldn't play basketball during free time was considered almost subhuman. I was called names and picked on constantly by the more athletically inclined who would target my small group of friends who mostly sat on the sidelines after calisthenics. We were the objects of constant derision almost throughout the three years of junior high school from 7th through 9th grade.

Until . . .

One Spring night, at age 14, at around 3:00 in the morning, I began to hear words in my head, narrated as if by Bob Dylan, of what soon became known simply as "The Drug Poem."

Unable to sleep, I went out to the Living Room and began to write. What came out was a gritty set of verses about heroin addiction, and the sad story of a poor soul who eventually winds up in a methadone clinic feeling that much of his life had been wasted.

The school was having a 9th-grade poetry contest, so I entered it and read the drug poem, on stage, at the weekly assembly, before almost the entire student body. My reading got thunderous applause, and I won the contest (although the school's promised prize of a fifty-dollar U.S. Savings Bond to the winner never materialized).

This was during the early stages of America's "War on Drugs" and, apparently, I had shocked the audience with my passionate reading and delivery of the message. I think they also liked my emphatic use of the word "Hell," and my reference to a "pusher," as drug-dealers were called in those days. **In any event, from that moment on, miraculously, all**

the bullying stopped. I'll never forget my shock and delight when one of the students in the cafeteria actually *defended me* from an attack by a bully who was trying to give me a hard time:

> *"No, no, he's cool. Leave him alone!*
> *Didn't you hear his poem the other day?*
> *He's my MAN!"*

My life had changed overnight. If I were back in school today, it would undoubtedly have become a rap song:

"Larry's JHS Drug Poem" (1970, age 14)

I sit and I watch you all blowing your minds,
And I stare, and I wonder,
How you can all be so blind

How so many said, "I ain't scared,
I'll just try once for kicks,"
One month later, your out robbing,
Just to get your next fix!

You look for someone to turn to,
You say the "pusher's a liar!"
And he tells you it's your fault,
Because you're the buyer.

There's a burning in your head
but no money left to burn,
You feel empty, and aching,
With nowhere to turn,

You look all around for someone,
Where the Hell to hang the blame??
And to make it worse, you need more stuff,
Or else you'll go insane.

Your cry out to the world,
But you get no reply,
You scream,
"Somebody help me or I'm sure I will die!!"

You wish you could wake up,
And forget you exist,
Your skin is pale, your lips are numb,
So you shove 'em with your fist,

The blood runs down,
You don't know it,
Cause your tongue don't work too well,

You fall unconscious on the street,
And you wake up IN A CELL!!
You look around, you scream,
And then your curse yourself to Hell!

You don't know how you got there,
But you're sure the cop's a louse,
Then you get "lucky," they have "sympathy,"
And they put you in a House.
There's rows of beds with other guys,
Who all are just like you,
Then a lady walks into the room and says,
"How do you do?"

She names a whole long list of names,
And you think you hear yourself,
Then she takes a bottle marked "Methadone"
From way up on a shelf.

She jabs another needle in your arm,
She says you'll come to no more harm,
You wake up in an hour or two,
You feel dizzy, and hungry too,
But at least some senses are back in you!

The doctor is there, but you feel all alone,
You're told your life depends on methadone,
Now you're a lucky one who made it back again,
But the outside world still won't take you in.

You have trouble finding any job,
So you join the unemployment mob,
And as you look back on your lousy life,
You wonder if you could've had a wife,

And you wish you'd listened to the guy,
Who said it's not that important,
To get a high.

Not bad for age 14, in my humble opinion.

By the time I got to high school, I started writing poetic pieces for friends, including inspirational ones, if they were discouraged or down in the dumps. One in particular that I recall was for a female friend who was feeling depressed and down on herself, perhaps over a failed relationship or a homework assignment that got a bad grade, or maybe a dispute with a teacher or classmate. Anyway, I remember her lamenting that she was suddenly riddled with doubts about herself, her self-worth as a friend, or even her value as a human being. I wrote her a confidence-building poem of which I can only recall that the latter part went something like this:

> *... You are not made up of your doubts,*
> *But of the power of your assurances.*
> *Your doubts are but umbrellas*
> *against the rainfall that is you*
> *They try to stop it,*
> *they try to block it out,*
> *But they can never really alter its power,*
>
> *And you need only to reach out your hand,*
> *Only to look up,*
> *To know that it is still raining...*
> *And with a force that can make*
> *anything it touches*
> *Beautifully wet.*

She was touched and heartened by it, and I remember feeling that the words had hit their mark. They had communicated something that I felt I never could have said with mere conversation, nor even with an hours-long heart-to-heart pep talk. She gave me a big hug and a kiss, and I was hooked!

There was a satisfaction in that moment which I will never forget. I felt grateful and proud at the same time, for I had been guided by my own compassion (not to mention some attraction to the girl) to write something that was genuinely helpful to another, and not just as a way of showing off what I was starting to feel *might* be a talent.

I was, therefore, feeling confident when, in my freshman year of college, I came in for an interview with a professor who was teaching a poetry-writing course at the school. He asked me what my personal definition of poetry was, and I told him a favorite quote I had recently read which defined it thusly: ***"Poetry is a language that tells us, through a more or less emotional reaction, something which cannot be said."*** (I've since learned that this quote came from a poet named Edwin Arlington Robinson, in a *1916 New York Times* interview with Joyce Kilmer.)

I walked in, armed with a few or my poems, some of which I had thought of as being my best. He read them quickly and summarily dismissed them as not being poetry at all. He gave me a list of poets to study if I wanted to see "what real poetry was," and said that if I ever wanted to make it in *his* class, I would have to throw out all of my ideas of what poetry was, and start over from scratch! I took his list and I went to the campus library to take out books by the poets he recommended.

I did not like any of them. I found them pretentious, overly flowery, and filled with obscure turns of phrase that seemed deliberately obtuse and hard to grasp. I withdrew from that course. Nevertheless, I decided for several years that if my stuff was not to be considered poetry by a "poet's poet," I would stick to writing prose pieces, and so I continued to do well with essays and creative writing classes. It was not until several years later that I allowed myself to dare to dip my toe, once again, "into the waters of the poetry pool."

Most of my poems of the last couple of decades have come out what I call "spiritual insight," as they tend to reflect my personal experience with the concepts of Eastern metaphysical philosophy (something I actually began studying during that same fateful freshman year), as well as with interfaith concepts and ideas about our common humanity. I've continued as a student of yoga and Indian spiritual thought, in one form or another, since the mid-1970s, and have also been influenced by my studies at an interfaith seminary since having been ordained as an interfaith minister in 2011, and then continuing to work for the seminary ever since, in the capacity of its "Media Manager," facilitating video class recording, editing, and distribution to students, faculty, and guest speakers. This has given me the opportunity to meet several great teachers from many spiritual traditions, as well as the brilliant and inspired students who continue to come year after year. In fact, many of those who have encouraged me to put this book together have been teachers and fellow alumni of All Faiths Seminary International.

A good number of these pieces come to me in rhyming verse, while some, like the "Conscious Constitution" may not really qualify as a poem at all by most standards, though it certainly takes poetic license in combining Eastern spiritual concepts with a sort of a mash-up of elements of the *Constitution of the United States,* and the *Gettysburg Address.*

These renderings are gleaned from life, as expressions of personal—mostly inner—experience, rather than rehashing any specifics learned from books or teachers. They reflect themes, events, and musings that became so strong as to bid me to commit them to this form, and now to share them. It is my hope that some of them, at least, resonate with readers.

–Larry

Namaskar

I bow to The Source of All

I bow to the One Lord of the Universe,
Who is Beyond All Names and Forms,
yet is worshipped by many
    in many different names and forms,

I bow to the One True God,
Who is Beyond All Religions,
yet is at the root of all religions
I bow to the One Who Knows (no matter what names are used),
Who He Is
Who She Is
Who It Is
Who I Am,
Who ALL are,
yet who is not fully known by any one human category
And cannot be fully known by any of them

I bow to the One known as Creator, Sustainer, Father,
Mother, Destroyer, Savior, Friend, Regenerator,
and Cosmic Dancer...

All Creation is your Dance
All dramas are your play
All beliefs are ideas within You
Without the Dancer, there is no Dance

I bow to the One Consciousness pervading All
Which contains all our limited forms of consciousness,
and without whom all would be
unconscious.

I bow to the One
whose laws are impossible to break,
The laws of *nature* are your laws
The laws of *science* are your laws
All action takes place *within* Your laws

All other laws are but diluted echoes
of the idea underlying this conscious
ongoing creation.

I bow to the TRUTH.

Self-Inquiry

Sometimes I am everything,
And sometimes I'm just me,
What inside decides to act,
And what part lets it be?

What part in me writes the poem,
And what part of it reads?
What part of me eats the food,
And who is it that feeds?

What part just sits idly by,
To radiate or shine?
And who is it that reads these words,
And who decides "they're *mine*"?

Who that likes the melodrama,
Who incurs the debts of karma?
Who goes crying for his mama
Who that stays serene and calmer?

Who takes the body here and there,
And sees and tastes it all?
Who knows that it is vastness?
Who complains it's very small?

Who decides it wants the food,
And who reports that it is good?
Who just sees the movie run but never is a critic
And who's mind is it anyway that gets so analytic?

If no one is the watcher,
The enjoyer, or the jerk,

Then who is it that tells him that he still "needs lots of work?"

Who remains the silent one
Not even as an "I"?
And who decides to play, talk, interact,
Identify?

The play's the thing,
When so inclined,
To catch the conscience of the mind
Who says "I know—it rang so true…
While sitting in satsang with you?
Who says nothing,
Not a sound
Is everywhere,
Formless, unbound?

Who knows when there's "no one home"
Who watches all with glee?
And who is it picks up the phone,
And says: "Hello, it's me."?

Silently together,
Or noisily alone,
Something sits inside to watch,
And something writes the poem,

And wonders just how it can be:
The silent witness
And the me…

When the eyes are all just mirrors
Looking back at this one Self,
Who feels sometimes like a giant,

The Conscious Constitution
(OR: *The Constitution of the United States of Consciousness*)

*Four score and a millennia ago, "Me," the Awareness of the
Conscious States,
in order to form a more Perfect Union, embarked upon a journey
and set forth upon this Planet, a new incarnation.*

*Conceived in Liberty, and Dedicated to the proposition that all
sentients are created equal, and that they are endowed by their
Creator with certain inalienable rights, and that among these are
Life everlasting,
Liberty from the cycle of births and deaths, and the pursuit of
Supreme Happiness.*

And that
*Whenever any state or condition arises that threatens to thwart these
rights,
their goal shall be pursued through sadhana, or dedicated
spiritually-oriented practice of some kind, and the adoption of an
attitude of compassion to ourselves and our posterity, our fellows—
brothers and sisters on this material plane—and in the recognition
that all beings are somewhere along the continuum of this endless
cycle, inhabiting the place where we have been, just were, or would
still be without the Grace of God—the Creative and Sustaining
Force, and that in this interrelating process, any one of us may at
some point rise to that level of vision from which he or she could
see that All of Us, simultaneously and without distinction, are
participating fully in this game of Being, from one or more of the*

infinite varieties or conditions in which this Selfsame Awareness
may find itself at any given moment.

And that
To deny these rights to the illusion of "others" is truly to deny an
aspect of our own condition, equally existent
but ultimately unreal, vibrating at just another frequency of
the evolutionary expression that spreads across the spectrum of
manifestation, from dreams to subjectively solid existence, through
all the endless combinations
and interdependent constellations of experience and relativity
ranging through the universe,
as they arise, move, act, and interact as the individuals we generally
agree that we are
and perceive ourselves to be.

And if
For any reason whatsoever, an "individual" shall deny these
Truths, that aspect of being shall be limited to the perception of
separateness to that extent to which he or she believes it to be so,
and for the duration of that belief and its interdependent substrata
of conscious and unconscious thought and action, and for however
long it takes for the unfolding events of that being's set of lives and
circumstances to come to a resolution of these limiting beliefs, and to
once again embrace the Reality that We are All One, indivisible and
everlasting, and shall not perish from the Heavens and the Earth.

Satsang

All of us are welcome here,
All the love and all the fear,
All the conflicts, all the hopes,
Hanging by belief's old ropes,
Welcome falsehoods,
Welcome facts,
Melting the whole ball of wax,
at the satsang of the Self.

Welcome to our meditations,
Welcome too, our limitations,
Welcome feelings,
Welcome pains,
Drying heat and drenching rains,
Welcome clean, and welcome stains,
Welcome floods and sewage drains,

Welcome worship of all strains.
Welcome religious forms—all poses,
Krishna, Jesus, Mohammed, Moses,
Nature itself, the woods and roses,
Mother, Goddess—whatever shows is ...

Arising to fill our beliefs and thinking,
With structures: sustaining, loving, linking.

Awareness expands,
Accepts what is,
Including all the "blockages"
Going on, it doesn't cease,
The noise exists in quiet peace.

All is welcome,
None left out,
Welcome silence, song, and shout,
Endless Ocean,
God and Being,
Ongoing waves of you and me-ing

All dissolves,
To gently see
Its Origin, Infinity

Fast and slow, and right and wrong,
We've been dancing for so long,
It stops while moving,
It sings while quiet,
It loves us all:
Your "it" and my "it"

Nothing to shrink from,
All is Welcome,
Let Heaven come,
But so let Hell come...
The rambling of the paranoid,
The Christian Love,
The Buddhist void,
The Jewish heart,
The monk's sheer piety,
And bawdy irreverence
Of every variety

It loves as God,
It sees as "I"
It holds as "your,"
It holds as "my"

We know of sorrow,
But keep it not,
Welcome it all
To the melting pot,
All the figures, all the facts,
Dissolving the whole ball of wax,
In the satsang of I Am.

On Blind Faith

When religion is based on fear, not Love,
You cannot feel that God's within,
You're stuck with the fear of "that God above,"
And spend your days in dreading "sin,"

You feel threatened that folks outside
Will obscure the "divine truth" from others,
And cannot see it's not they who hide,
The Oneness you share with all sisters and brothers,

You cling to verses in a book,
And dare not go within yourself,
You cannot take that deeper look,
When you put the book up on the shelf,

The darkest fears then make you tell,
All sorts of lies you think are real,
You'd rather say, "Kill the infidel!"
Than see inside behind your zeal,
Plowing Heaven under, creating "hell,"
You run from what you cannot feel,

And while obsessed with hatred and killing,
Far from the Truth behind your chapter and verse,
Seeing only difference in those unwilling
To follow your way, you make things worse.

Wars, and famines—the years roll by,
Generations of blood spilled on the soil,
As families torn apart moan and cry,
From the folly of your misguided toil,

When you say, "My way or the highway,"
Proclaiming God bids you to carry that torch,
You block the very Light of day,
And cast long shadows o'er the Earth you scorch,

Whether Hindu, Muslim, Christian or Jew,
The subtle music of your soul:
Singing *Never instead, but in addition to*
Is the song that could have made you whole.

This refrain down through the ages,
Missed by zealots in their furious blindness,
Yet heard by saints, rishis, and sages,
Could have turned the world
Into one of kindness.

In every age, the flame of Truth burns,
Obscured by those who see only its smoke,
And heads keep spinning as the world turns...
A blind eye and deaf ear to the
Seers who spoke...

...But what if it Still is not too late,
To Listen to that "Still small voice within"?
Still to *turn* toward Love, and away from hate,
And Still that violent, negative spin?

Can the world yet come to Peace,
Without condemnation and invective?
With real understanding, violence will cease,
Grasping difference as being
only in perspective.

This then is our fervent prayer—
A Cause to sing an anthem by:
Listen WELL to the Inner Love and Care,
Let that "still small voice" be ***AMPLIFIED!!***

If actions do speak louder than words,
And if we act from the inner Heart,
It will take time but it's not absurd,
To give peace a chance,
And *NOW's* the time to *Start!*

A Lila's Odyssey *(a ballad for soul-mates)*

Surrounded by a circle of time,
>two loving souls stepped up to their line,
They'd known each other in a time before,
>but their love uncompleted, they returned for more.
Married through time in multiples of space,
>running homeward, treading Maya's delusional pace,
Deep within them, imprinted, what miles to trod,
>magnetized for approach: Together, Towards God.
Yet ever along on their mystical flight,
>Maya's steeds come, undaunted, distorting their light,
One after another, at gallop or trot,
>telling each of our lovers they are something they're not.

Through lifetimes and deathtimes, they've been chained by this bind:
>*Karmas made in one realm, to be made up in kind...*
...Now they're merging in space... now they first see the linkage...
>...amidst bodies, and minds, and sensations, and *thinkage!*

Yet onward they race toward the Lord of their quest,
>tripping or running through test after test,
At times overwhelmed by the struggles and pains,
>they lose sight of their love,
They lose hold of the reins!

They feel lost...

    disconnected,
like...

        ...two...

          ... severed...

            ... entities...

In the tangled mane of Maya, lies their Divine Identity.

Yet where miracles are commonplace,
At the Source of each soul,
Sits the Heavenly Father, The Mother, The Goal,
Saying: "Come on to Me, Though you dance as you do,
Through my *Lilas,* my games, I'm still pulling you through,"
Through the detours and pitfalls,
Through the miles to trod...
march two souls, ever-matched,
Towards their matchmaker, God.

A Prayer Poem

So where've you been, Larry?

I've been through a mini dark-night of the soul...

Are you back yet?

I don't know. I still don't feel quite whole.

Something's missing and something's changed.
Something's opened, and some things rearranged.
There's a real need to rely on Faith and on Trust,
and perceiving that behind doubt and fear, there's a *MUST*...

But what it is that *MUST* come, I do not quite know,
I surrender my heart in a prayer: *Let it show,*
and illumine my mind and refresh my weary bod,
Cause whatever it is, I know it's coming from God.

If I can only stay empty I'll feel what is next,
Giving up trying and straining, perplexed.
Having opened my soul as best as I am able,
May Wisdom and Assurance settle in and be stable.

It will come from inside me, the wellspring runs deep,
In the seat of my soul, in Divinity's keep.
The True Self, the Knower, the I AM inside,
That my foolish mind seems to for*get* and to hide.

If I ever get tired of playing this game,
I'll be wise beyond measure, and reflect the same,
I'll see the same beauty in each one of you,
And get out of my own way and let the Love through.

In the meantime I'm tired, tripping over my laces,
Not always recognizing the Divine in all faces,
There's still something left, something not quite outgrown,
That can't see It in your face—or even my own!

But whenever It shines through, I steadfastly pray,
May I just remember not to get in Its way,
And surrender enough so It will finally stay,
May It hold you, and keep you, and Lighten your way.

A Work in Progress

From Columbine to Connecticut,
We've seen these things arise,
Are we as humans in a rut,
Far from Light and clearer skies?
Can Love be our response to hate,
When darkness clouds another's eyes?
And can we help the pain abate,
While the innocent bleed and the child dies?
The news grabs us, makes us stop,
Yet seems to come now ever faster,
We hear in awe, we cry in shock...
At killings, famine, war, disaster
From far away to right at home,
Murder, earthquake, flood, and fire,
We question what our part can be,
In situations unplanned and dire.
From New Orleans to Jap*an,*
Asia to Haiti, L.A. to New York,
The heartbreak of our fellow man,
we cry, we stop, can't even talk,
Do we break the silence? Do we even dare?
And how to do so if we can?
When tears on graves, lie fresh and bare,
Over children who died even whilst they ran?
As these disasters come and go,
Some wonder if it's all a test,
Our fellow humans suffer so,
How can we simply hear and rest?

Compassion binding us together
Awakens Love to ease the friction,
In our separate lives, it is the tether,
When truth seems now,
More strange than fiction.
We start to feel that we are one,
With troubled souls so close before us,
In reaching out, then, it's begun,
Let's join our Love in powerful chorus
Demonstrating more than power,
Is what's prevailed throughout the ages,
Feeling our common goals this hour,
Connects and heals as Love engages.
Life itself becomes the bond,
When recognized for all its worth,
It's *Love* of which we all are fond,
That inner sense instilled since birth,
Even as tragedy brings us close,
That very closeness is the key,
We survive as each of us sees and knows,

We're all part of One Human Family.

Terrorist Kids

"Why do they hate us so much?"

The truth is that they don't.

They don't hate *us*.
They hate the lie that they have been told that we are.
They hate the boogey-man, just as all children do,
      but they have been told that he is flesh-and-blood and lives in America.
They have been taught since they were small that they can shoot him and win,
      even if they die in the process.

They cheer when they see his castles come falling down.
They pick up their weapons like toys and shout *hooray* that the evil giants' village
      is starting to fall from the sky.
They wait for our planes to fly overhead to give them target practice.
They wait for our soldiers to land on their soil so they can see what color the boogey-man's blood really is.
They have been taught since childhood that if they die when they fight him, they will surely go to Heaven, a much, much better place than where they live now.

So they wait for the opportunity to move to the bright new neighborhood.
To die in the battle is to win the war. It is a one-way ticket out of Hell—
      the only neighborhood they have ever known.
They cannot see our children and families grieving, our hearts and minds torn asunder,

They cannot taste our tears nor hear the laughter they have silenced.
Ours is a way of life they cannot even imagine, nor the fear of the threat they
     pose to it.
They don't know who we are. They cannot even see us.
They don't hate **us.**

Why, Oh, Why?

Why do we play a game that's painful?
Mean, or hurtful, or disdainful?
Why have feelings so wax- and waneful,
As if being ourselves was somehow shameful?

Why do our hearts play hide and seek
With minds unsteady, frail, or meek?

We put ourselves through needless stress
Believing that we must pass a test...

In truth we're fine just as we are,
No less than mountain, bird, or star,
Or leaf or flower, which surely wilt,
And yet are never wracked with guilt.

Why, Oh, why do we play this game...
When in our hearts we're all the same?

Perhaps I could've called this "When & Where We Get Stuck."
. . . Anyway, I guess we all find ourselves at this juncture from time
to time, when we are honest enough with ourselves to admit it . . .

A Place to Pause

I came upon a crossroads,
After wandering many years,
One way lay transcendence,
The other through the "veil of tears."

One would lead me up so high,
A widerange map revealing all,
The other, strewn with obstacles,
 to release, to mend, to heal and cry,

With steadfast faith I'd surely rise,
Along the path to lofty heights,
Balancing through inner skies,
Beyond all maybes, doubts, and frights.

The other flowed through all the knots,
Of friends, commitments, peers, relations,
Melting, shedding all that rots,
With emotion, care, and contemplation.

Stumbling to the end, I'd see,
my life's work through with strengthened bonds,
I'd come through clean but still as me,
And rest on shores of clearer ponds

The higher path would leave behind
All aspirations, thoughts and plans,
Releasing all ideas of mind,
Past chartered oceans, space, or lands.

Inner paths shallow and steep:
Enough to make me stop and wonder,
From heights might I yet still fall deep,
Transcendent maps then torn asunder?

In throwing caution to the winds,
Would I soar upon them flying,
Or fall into a new abyss,
Of pointlessness and futile trying?

And were the choices only two:
To risk it all, perchance to fly?
Or carve my way on Earth below,
Mending fences until I die?

In need, I had to stop and rest,
Neither loosing all bonds nor proceeding to heal,
No sobbing came to pass the test,
While for flying, I yet lacked the zeal.

I lingered at the point between,
With neither faith's courage nor pressing fears,
Not, sobbing, not flying, neither wretched, nor clean,
On the crossroads of transcendence and the "veil of tears."

On Conservation of the Immaterial...

The fact is true while we exist,
We persist in doing
What we can't resist

Tolerance wanes and tolerance waxes,
It increases when our ego relaxes,
When we cannot resist temptation,
It helps to sit for meditation

So many things that seem so nice
Come at a later but costly price
And so we grow and so we learn,
We lose what we cling to,
We release what we earn

The paradox of ash remaining
What doesn't burn is more sustaining,
In letting go, we find, down deep,
Something more powerful, in silence to keep

And see in all the outer reflection
The facets of our own perfection
We sit, we study, we sing, we try
To still our wings so they spread to fly.

Recollection

Existing in a nonverbal state,
words were available as expression
not pondered over by mental effort
but springing from that inner understanding,
Always knowing what I know
without vain attempts to recall or reiterate
That which was already known

I am a human being.
We do not have to keep reminding ourselves;
It is common knowledge, as was everything else,
and when the need to communicate arose,
the words would rise from within to meet an other's mind
measured before they were formed, not merely before they are uttered.

Almost floating, being within the calm of knowing oneself,
They were in the service of the idea, in the service of the situation,
they came unbeckoned, the mind was their servant
of expression only.

Communication was surprising sometimes,
sensing the apparent complexity required
to convey such a radically simple source
of an idea in such ways that another mind
could grasp what lay behind them

Now, too often, I struggle to recollect
not the bits and pieces of a scattered collection
but the very essence from which it sprang
simple and knowing, understood and known
prior to its representation as separate ideas

The common thread of all things
seems to get lost in the translation,
of linguistic gymnastics.
both inner and outer,
as if the need to say is now internalized
by some unseeing mind
which grasps at holding an identity never really its own.

To let go of this is to live spontaneously
from the heart,
from the soul,
from essential nature
from the One within

Despite knowing it has never really gone anywhere,
 the outer circumstances seem to shape me
into reacting from fear
of knowing not how I will survive,
work, earn, eat, provide, offer service,
indeed continue as myself
in a world seeming crushingly overburdening

With skills obsolete, learning slowed,
    false identifications, and worries made not in the service of the
Self, but of the fear of not knowing it.

What are we humans that we fear our own demise
in such a pretense that we hasten its onset?
As if fear itself could envelop the Truth
of all we always are,
obscuring essence from mind
in a dance designed by a mad choreographer?

Ommm... the mantras sprang not into memory
but from the essence behind it, behind all,
Not formulas for recollection,
but the melodies of the soul emerging from its slumber,
Expressing themselves in joyful inward to outward flow,
not as strivings to remind the mind, trying to lead it back to its original
quietude

O, to live in the knowledge all the time...!
We are one, and from oneness we connect.
When this recollection really takes place,
it is the opposite of an event.
It is the very meaning which gives events their meaning
and communication is
and understanding stands,
and Love is shared,
and comprehended.

A Trick of Mind

A trick of mind
To help us shed
Our false identity:
Stop being a person who...
And instead,
Just *Be*.

Aftershocks: A Disaster Poem

Through the course of millennia, a pattern lingers,
Recurring again in our own times,
from ancient bells to cellphone ringers,
An alarming sound in its echoes and chimes:

While seeking personal glory or fame,
And seeing ourselves as mere sinew and phlegm,
Atrocities committed in the name,
Of religions declared as deadset against them.

Still the drama unfolds yet again and again,
During earthquakes and floods and calamitous weather,
Common plight can be seen by our family of man,
And it softens and moves us and binds us together.

Does it take a natural disaster,
Breaking our hearts and instilling a cause,
To enliven compassion and bond us then faster
To embody mercy, and overlook flaws?

When a human enemy cannot be condemned,
For deliberate acts of bloodshed or cruelness,
Is tragedy only Fate's power to mend?
And to rally our hearts in a cauldron that fuels us?

In the absence of blessings, we pool our resources
While perceiving, arising among us, a sense,
That the "lesson" of bounties declining, "of course," is
To blame our disasters on Providence!

Yet when we can see how such pain begets Love,
In a space that till recently held only fear,
Are we not moved to carry that bold and less thought of...
...idea that our enemies lives can seem dear?

So let us neither curse the Fates,
Nor blame an unjust Lord of Decree,
Let's maintain the bonds and lose the hate,
And keep on Loving tenderly

It doesn't matter which came first,
Chicken or egg, fear or magic,
Compassion in disaster can quench a thirst
Let's sustain the Love after the tragic.

Paradox

Such a paradox You have shown me,
That it is only at your Feet,
That I will see your Face,
And then, when you show it to me,
It is My Own.

Gender Equality

Genuinely gender-free,
Without forced "him, her, they, or she,"
Would be a pleasant victory, away from all hypocrisy.

Though bigotry can be quite brutal,
Pushing pronouns seems quite futile,
In changing minds of those who may
Attack those trans, bi, straight, or gay,
For simply living or loving that way!

[Political] spin, volatility, and idolatry
Can pre-empt the achievement of true equality,
Leading into more hostility
By those who can't or will not see

The Truth, though, some may find it odd,
The real gender-neutral one is God!
If we're truly made in the image of
The Omnipresence we claim to Love,

It will take more than pronouns to set things right,
And for everyone to see the Light,
For true equity to come to pass,
And usher a global change, *en masse,*

Insight cannot be stipulated,
Legislated, or regulated,
Liberty will not be hastened
Just because those who hate are chastened.

Compassion has to arise within
The hearts of those who see a sin
In folks just being what they've always been,
In a world still plagued by brutality
For lacking gender-neutrality.

Awareness

Awareness
Is

THIS is.

What is this business of Isness?

Awareness is This.
This is Awareness.

What is THIS?
The experience of existing as itself.

Is "I" THIS?

Am "I" that which is Aware?

"I" strikes "me" as being identity.
after pure "THISness."

THIS is.

Always...

Eye of God

It opens and closes again and again,
The Wisdom of God and the vision of men,
But what do we see when we look through these eyes?
Do we repeat the spiral or find a surprise?

How long do we wander?
How long do we yearn?
When we're sometimes so close
And sometimes we just burn?

For thousands of years we've been doing this dance,
War, inspiration, religion, romance,
While the glimpses within that we get in between,
Are unveiling the Truth beyond all these extremes

A faith in the stillness must come to arise,
Recognizing that small point that's almost disguised,
Peace behind chaos, behind sadness and grief
If focused upon can, in time, bring relief

The dance still goes on and our lives will progress,
In circles and spirals along with the rest,
Knowing this we can then have compassion for all,
In the same boat we rise, or we sink, or we fall

Can the antidote for the seeming futility
Be simple Loving-kindness and acts of humility?
Let's try it and find out. Let's practice and see
If compassion and Love really can set us free.

Confession (in Mixed Verse

So what happens if I "confess"
that I'm a nondualist,

Yet feel compassion for all?

Will I be shunned as a hypocrite
whenever
I lose my temper?

Or start to savor
"slipups" into selfish behavior?

When the ego "gets the best of me,"
And I fall on my face
(over and over),
Will I rest in that place?
Say the ground's sweet with clover?

Will I marvel at my pain, Discomfort, and joy?
Will I land and stand like a man who's grand?
Or cry like a boy saying, "Oy, oy, oy, oy!!!"?

And if I fail,
Even land in jail,
With no one there to pay my bail,
Will I go within and study Truth,
Or feel lonely, unloved,
Trapped and stuck in a booth?

Either way,
However it plays out,
Like all of us,
I'll live my days out.

And if it doesn't matter in the end,
I'll still be glad to call you friend.

Paradigm Shift

We have to be willing to let boundaries go
Snip the edges where the suit confines,
And see how we expand into greater lines

If it gets uncomfortable
When push comes to shove
Then we must choose discomfort
In the name of Love.

When old beliefs begin to crumble
because of conflicting facts
we must realign our mental blocks
in order to once again relax

It may be obvious and enormous
Or may pivot on something more slight than a dime
Which when recognized creates a shift
 in our personal space and time

We must go on but not as before,
Allowing a settling-in required,
Before we can integrate into our lives,
the facts that some belief expired

No forcing square pieces into round holes
will suffice to go on from this point
We have to fit right where we stand,
a new paradigm to appoint

Love Poem (09/10/2016)

In spite of depression,
The Love is there,
In spite of fear,
The Love carries us through,
It sustains us,
Maintains us,
Blesses us from within,
Shows Itself in each other's eyes,
Shines from within each other's hearts,
Connects us to each other's souls,
Takes us to wherever we are going next...

It never fades,
It never wavers,
It never leaves us,
We are never alone.

That Love is the ocean in which we float,
The ground on which we walk,
The air in which we breathe,
The nourisher in what we eat,

That Love is the river of destiny
On which we float,
The light in which we see,
The music in all we hear,
The vehicle by which we move,
And the bed in which we rest.

The Divinity in which we pray,
The Formless presence in which we worship.

It flows through our veins,
Enlivens our passions,
Buoys us through stormy times,
And radiates inwardly as Peace.

It is the knower of our knowledge,
The keeper of our memories,
The teller of our stories,
The true goal of our desires,
The resting place of all striving,
The reward of all efforts,
The placeholder of our progress,
The reality behind our identities.
And the end of all beginnings,
As well as their Source.

We are blessed to have been cast,
In this play of Living,
With the deathless Love,
So evident and forgiving.

Every day I give thanks,
That it has shown itself to me,
In your face.

Love Poem (09/10/2017)

Beyond the mind,
And beyond all fear,
Is a Love that's been with you
Since your very first year,

It's what I first saw in your eyes,
When I beheld you under sunny skies,
Deep in the heart and behind all thoughts,
Beneath the chatter, shoulds, and oughts,

Infused throughout, in blood and flesh,
Instilled in action, causing all to mesh,
Present even when all seems lost,
But never gone at any cost,

Carried on by every breath,
Of Life itself, and on through death,
Forever indwelling at the core,
Beyond time and space and more,

Love itself is radiating,
Through mournful times, and celebrating,
And when we're quiet enough to link,
With this power greater than all that we think,

We ride it like a silent wave,
Surfing on tides we needn't save,
For the Ocean of Love is vaster than,
Any thoughts of woman, child, or man,

The surf continues as we ride,
As wave, or ripple, current or tide,
You and me, and all inside,
Past anywhere it seems to hide,

Animal, microbe, fish, or plant,
And back to you, as you just can't
Be anything other than the Love you are,
Within your heartCit isn't far,

Within these walls,
Below this ceiling,
Dwells this Love surpassing feeling,
More than enough for all you do,
For this I've seen myself,
in you.

Valentine's Day, 2017

Between plotting one's destiny
And going with the flow
Is a point where even time
Ceases to go

A realm beyond reason
And far beyond rhyme,
beyond waves of karma,
and the currents of time,

Past the point of decision,
and the currents of fates,
remains Love,
glowing silently,
drawing in mates

Magnetic attraction
to which we respond
Arranging our choosing
To honor the bond,

An ancient melody
playing its themes
on the cusp of reality
merging with dreams

While we live our lives

Wondering if right or wrong,
We're occasionally graced
to catch a snippet of Song

Is it something we hear,
or something we sing?
Emanation of All,
And a story we bring

When blessed to find Love,
In each other's eyes,
To manifest or succumb...?
What lets us harmonize?

Surrendering to Love,
The only attitude,
to navigate blessings
in true gratitude.

Here where Love holds us,
Beyond time and space,
Beyond movement and stillness
Is the presence of Grace.

Monism

Monotheism
Presents a schism:
If indeed there is one God,
Does He also exist within the bod?

If God is truly omnipresent,
Is He not within tree, bird, mouse, and peasant?

If nothing was first, before the Divine,
Before the Big Bang of Creation,
Then out of That came every thing
Yours, hers, his, mine,
Of every station.

All the isms, all belief,
Sage and student, cop and thief,
Are permeated with that Love,
Beyond what we've all been thinking of,

Beyond our thoughts, our hopes, our dreams,
Divinity's stitching, stuffing, and seams,
Our hearts and minds,
Our very core,
All we have done and what's in store,

One is her, and one is him,
A glorious Godly Monism,
Every part infused with Light,
So what's to fear? And why the fright?

Divinity in our very being,
All it does, and all we're seeing,
Is the ever Cosmic Dance
From single atom to great romance.

So sing and play, and work and rest
We've all already passed the "test,"
It was never even ours to fail,
And only God's left to prevail.

My Own Impatience

With all the knowledge I possess,
I still get impatient with the process,

When contraction comes to mind,
with thoughts or resentments,
that seem unkind,

When the first reaction is thinking of
ideas that seem far less than Love,

Toward those I hold so very dear,
yet react with annoyance, anger, or fear,

It's then that I have a chance to choose,
to let go of reacting so as not to lose

Sight of the tenderness deep in the heart,
That's always within, right from the start,

Can I watch as such feelings dissolve,
And so the tensions just resolve?

Or is there more "work" I must do
To quell the reaction and see it through?

I seek forgiveness, inner and outer,
To avoid becoming the reactive shouter

That masquerades as self-righteousness,
clouding my vision and consciousness

And knowing that this too shall pass,
Though it lingers and doesn't go too fast,

Diving deep, the Love is there,
even when folks seem to get in my hair

"I Love you. I'm sorry," seems all I can say,
When such roadblocks get in the way,

I will accept by Morning's Light,
That all is once again all right,

And knowing in truth that it always was,
Despite the mental clouds and fuzz,
Staying centered in the heart,
Grateful for every new fresh start.

Let us greet the dawn together
knowing such moods are just passing weather.

Needs

The outer needs the inner,
The micro needs the macro,
The surface needs the center,
The shallow needs the deep,
The ego needs the Self,
The wave needs the ocean,
The ignorant need the wise,
The devotee needs the deity,
The darkness needs the light...

The Absolute needs nothing.
Both All and Nothing are already within It.

On Inclusive Consciousness

Some say that Pure Consciousness
Is uninvolved, always at rest

That it's only we who "dream the dream"
Of things being or not beingwhat they seem

Like a movie's white light behind what's projected,
The highest truth remains unaffected

Yet if God's presence has veracity
Is not feeling our feelings within His capacity?

To limit the infinitely Absolute
To the noninteractive resolute

May be a way for us to dare
To say "God doesn't *DO,* and doesn't care"

The Dance goes on, and every dancer
Lives his dream as a romancer

I Sense somehow that the real fact is
The full experience of every act is

Part and parcel of the whole
The world, the cosmos, and the soul

One without the other is lame

An empty board, a playerless game

I choose to say, and be effusive
That Divinity is more inclusive

Of all that we have yet perceived,
Or lived, experienced, or believed

Everything that can enthrall
The One in many includes them all

Allowing every concept a place
In Universal Infinite Space

Formless & form, aware of each other
Distant son, empathic mother

All in all in all in all,
I cannot limit God at all

On Stopping Thoughts

There's a place within
When thoughts reach a slowness,
Where we stop and say, "Wait—
I already know this.

I need not repeat it again & again,
It's as clear as the back of my hand,
Or my name."

When we get there, don't question,
Just rest in the knowing,
That returning to this place
Is the seed of all growing.

Herein lies the Truth,
It's the door to fruition,
Remembering Wisdom
And true recognition.

When we can suspend our identification
With thoughts and old tapes,
It's a true liberation

What comes to the surface,
Eventually,
Is the I or the "eye"
we know *our*selves to be.

And in knowing ourselves,

We see *that* same in others,
Recognizing each other
As sisters and brothers

May we all be blessed
With that internal spin
To let go of our thoughts
For a real turn within.

Peace Poem (*written shortly after Sept. 11, 2001*)

This is not the time for pain,
Though feeling it, we must explain:
We needn't wallow in our sorrow,
But rise to build a new tomorrow

This is not the time for shame
But for coming together in the Name
of Love and Truth and Peace and Light,
Respect and Virtue, Good and Right,

There are those who pray to That as God,
And others still who find that odd;
For them to feel what makes us whole,
Let them reach out soul to soul,

And feel that force that makes us One,
Come on, just look!
It CAN be done...

The ways that tear and separate us
Turn brother on brother and make us hate us,
Are only the flipside of the coin,
Of the one cause we all must join

The light of human recognition

That each of us, in our position
Is fighting the very selfsame fight,
To know the truth and know the light,

The brother in the gutter there,
The sister in the easy chair,
The mother struggling to pay her bills,
The grandfather fighting his body's ills

All are you and all are me
Its plain as day if we but see
We *are* just one big family
With many roots on one huge tree

Those that deny it
Have only to try it
To open their hearts deep within to see,
That right there inside them
What can't be denied them,
We're all of the same consistency

It's those in pain who perpetrate
Acts of vengeance, violence, hate,
Flying rages against a nation,
Acts of wanton desperation
On those they see as beneath their station

And those of us who do resist

And stare at the sky and shake their fist
And cry that hatred and war exist
Eventually will be on the list

Of those in the great big family human,
Who give up all their gloom and doomin'
And love themselves enough to see
How war will finally cease to be

One day we'll tire of the game,
Of rights and wrongs and sin and shame,
And dropping it, shed our disguise,
And see ourselves in each other's eyes

Until that day when hate retires,
Some will live and some expire,
Some in peace and some by fighting,
But the prospect is exciting...

To try to live the Truth right here
Of what is common and what is dear
To all of us, both far and near
And what, in Light, becomes so clear

That what we see so deep within
That Divinity that we hold in,
Is waiting for us to see it through:
It's holding *us* in *It*self too

So remember as we go on,

and cheer and cherish, and weep and mourn,
The Source of Life in all we meet,
And smile at It on the street,

And know That One we all revere
Is right with all of us right here,
And right within them there as well
Is Heaven in the midst of Hell.

Schisms

Four people had the same dream,
But each remembered a different part,
One brought back music,
One mathematics,
One great writing,
The other art.

Each professed their cherished treasures
To the assembled in the public square,
Some sang, some read, some played, some drew,
While some calculated with precision and care.

Years passed and the village grew with them,
Each nurturing that to which most inclined,
And every year was a celebration,
Of the dream that inspired so many a mind.

The singers and players came together,
And harmonized under a beautiful arch,
Designed with the help of the mathematicians,
 who joined in their peaceful dance and march.

Still, some of the wordsmiths had the feeling,
That they couldn't quite get things right,
And pointing out differences rather than healing,
It all erupted into a fight!

They tried to turn for inspiration,
To the original four who had shared the dream,
But the meaning, obscured by opinionation,
left schisms instead of a common theme.

And so the town built separate churches,
each professing its personal creed,
Each favored one aspect over another,
But unable to say how they all agreed.

Silent Poem

Silence tells
mind stills
body listens,
does what comes next
So nice for mind not to have to work!

Knowledge is there
not by prompting
not by remembering
not by thinking
just by knowing
Where would it go?

When Silence rules the heart
The body listens
the mind rests
peace happens
the work gets done.

Existence
has
nowhere
else
to go.

Seeking Resonance

"I Seek Resonance."

Who seeks Resonance?
The ego.

What does it want to Resonate with?
The Self. The Truth.

How will it know when Resonance is achieved?
It will get out of its own way.

What will it feel?
It will feel itself recede into the background.

Can it stay?
Only as a bystander.

Will it see itself?
Only if it remains silent.

Will it come back?
As soon as it becomes noisy.

What will it do then?
It will seek Resonance.

The Search

When we seek the Truth, do we have a preference?
Are we seeking validation by established reference?

Are we willing to grope around in the dark,
Finding our way, only spark by spark?
Or do we seek the approval of friends,
Moving ever cautiously toward our ends?

Can we Love whatever we find,
Leaving cherished concepts and comfort behind?
Ready to let it be surprising,
Even when conflict or pain are rising?

We dream and struggle, and build our cocoon,
Thinking the effort can win us the moon,
But in what will we fly staying with the familiar?
Is the sky the dream of the caterpillar?
(Does the seed know the flower promised to the tiller?)

The embrace of the unknown is required,
We don't blossom when we feel too tired!
Stretching, expanding, making room,
Yielding pollen for butterfly and bloom ...

Keep dancing when we stub our toes,
The choreography comes and goes,
The paradox of willingness,
Uncovering nothing so thrilling as
The terror our own minds kept hidden,
Emerging now in light, unbidden,

Venturing out, safely exposed,
Spontaneous, no longer posed,
We're "out" with what we have released,
Once our fear of isolation's ceased,

Are we ready to take this ride,
Or must we wait till we've all but died
To take the journey out from inside,
While so many still prefer to hide?

When the time comes, we must let go,
Of cherished notions, fast and slow,
Discovering the sacred now,
In readiness to see and to allow.

On "Flawed Teachers"(?)

What if we didn't expect perfection,
If we started out saying we know that they're flawed?
Might it take us in a whole new direction...
To see what they offer that can yet leave us awed?

Knowing Divinity dwells within all,
Leaving room for surprises from those we might rate
As false gurus who crashed and were destined to fall,
Could these somehow "sub-par" ones
Then rise to seem great?

We learn from what reaches our own inner triggers
And fear what's perceived as just pushing us down
If a teacher has gone through such stuff,
Then it figures
We wonder: Will he help us to swim or to drown?

Do we turn our backs and say that one's disgraced,
And feel dirty and sullied, in need of a bath?
Or perhaps raise our sights and see all as just Grace,
Say: the Universe put that one here on our path?

Where do we feel we really learn
And what seems a detour, opposed to our dharma?
Can we examine what causes the burn,
Not blaming ourselves nor gurus for our karma?

In answering these questions, we must be quite frank,
Bluntly look in the mirror, alone, face to face,
It's our own inner journey,
We must fill in the blank:
What were lessons or pitfalls, and what's really Grace.

About the Author

LAWRENCE LEE SCHWARTZ (aka *Tzvi Hersch,* aka *Sitaram,* aka *Rev. Larry*) has been a student of yoga and Eastern philosophy as well as Western psychology since the mid-1970s. A Nursing student in the early 1980s, he completed his LPN license but decided that Nursing was not the profession for which he was most suited. He completed a bachelors degree in psychology in 1982, and, during the 1980s, stayed a few months at a time in yoga ashrams, in both the United States and India. Upon his return from his second trip to India in 1985, he worked at Showtime and the Movie Channel for three years as Operations Coordinator for their wholesale satellite division, and later for a brief stint as a copy editor for *NEWLIFE MAGAZINE.*

His life changed upon meeting his beloved wife, Tamar, in 1991, on a fateful walk through the New York Botanical Garden in his "hometown" of the Bronx (the couple wed in 1995). Shortly after, Larry learned a software program that allowed him became the typesetter for the *Journal of the American Psychoanalytic Association* (*JAPA*), on which he worked for 10 years, until he and Tamar began an independent publishing company known as IPBooks (see IPBooks.net), and also formed a business partnership.

In 2011, he enrolled in the interfaith seminary All Faiths Seminary International (see AllfaithsSeminary.org), and was ordained as an interfaith minister. He also began recording and distributing their monthly classes for the student body, faculty, and alumni—a position he has maintained to this day as the Media Manager for the school. Tamar and Larry continue their full-time work on IPBooks.net (now incorporated as IPBooks Inc) as well as facilitating conferences for mental health professionals, something they have also done since the late 1990s. For many years, they have also volunteered at a monthly soup kitchen (Mother's Kitchen) in New York City. Tamar and Larry work from their home in Sunnyside Queens, NY to which they moved after having lived in nearby Astoria, Queens for 26 years.

CPSIA information can be obtained
at www.ICGtesting.com
Printed in the USA
JSHW050757290622
27548JS00005B/130